T0356397

Inventorys offers a tour-de-force refusal of linguistic imperialism in six acts. Scattering syntax to the four winds, this awing debut collection excavates the wreckages of colonialism that remain embedded in our shorelines and our language use. Creely's text traces the trajectory of an eighteenth-century Spanish vessel to offer a threnody for the extracted resources and lifeworlds marked as "cargo" in the ship's manifest. Crystallizing around the figure of the cochineal insect whose red dyes would stain the sea, *Inventorys* sets the reader spinning in a tempestuous whorl of lexical items and attunes us to the multispecies distributions of colonial violence. At once elegiac and agitational, this book lingers with histories and presents that reject the imperative to move "forward into forgetting."
—Mashinka Firunts Hakopian, author of *The Institute for Other Intelligences*

When one tends what's near gone of history's "wreck and recovery," one dives deep to take account. Deep, yes: into love, into memory, into seas. Sam Creely's gorgeous and fleet *Inventorys* attends with tenderness that which, recovered, requires stitching into a once wounded whole of "hefted forms of replica." When what's lost resurfaces, washes ashore here, in this, their assured debut, Creely wrights it, eyeing its wrack, sets it thus, back into time, recording that yes, like a family line, the ocean is full of blood; yet there remains more red than that, "red enough for forgetting": read this to remember.
—Douglas Kearney, author of *Optic Subwoof*

Sam Creely's title *Inventorys* immediately shivers its signifier with an irregular plural that vibrates throughout this collection of poetry as it considers and reconsiders those philological and historical efforts to order and to control a fundamental condition of arbitrariness. The brilliant trope of inventory itself as a traumatic attempt to buffer the flow of production from the raw to the fabricated—from the noumenal to the phenomenal—and to ensure conventions of consumption and exchange is, paradoxically, the book's own lyrical economy.

From the Latin *inventum/inventus*, the etymology of "inventory" (like "invention") is of *a thing found; to have come upon*. It is, in a sense, to capitalize upon a discovery/recovery and to exploit its use value. This radical translation into textuality constantly risks its alienation from the animistic, so much so that the new constant becomes the constantly new, renewal only in progressive derealization. Implied is not only the fearsome logic of modernity and its ideologies of conquest and capital, of enlightenment and carnage, but the grief-stricken ravages of a personal search for lost time, of memory and melancholia within a history without end, a past that isn't even the past. "Taking inventory" characterizes an iteration without culmination, the constant slip and vertigo of identity and identification, of that "false lash."

The shipwreck of the 18th century Spanish colonial frigate El Nuevo Constante along with its monetized prize of cochineal is an almost too perfect metaphor for the flotsam of an age of synthetic rationality appearing as a stain upon the waters, returned from currency to ephemera and consigned to the mud of its own universalist logic. Creely's genius is to refine the historical epic into exile, into a dirge of loss become private ("Cochineal cradel me"), into the "Slow Rosebud" of a grandmother adrift in time. Off we go. In lines worthy of Eliot or Beckett, and in a critique worthy of Barthes, this collection, so singular in its periodicity, curates "what gathers behind words as they move into quiet, / how heavy how creased."
—Jon Wagner, translator, editor, and introducer of *Andrée Chedid: Fugitive Suns (Green Integer 37)*

Happily, when I unzipped the folder of the Omnidawn Open Book Contest semi-finalists, I discovered a number of manuscripts to which I might have with no qualms given the award; unhappily, of course, this meant I had to think hard before I settled upon a winner. But I'm glad I had to think hard—Sam Creely's *Inventorys* is a book that rewards thinking. Indeed, if you're anything like me, as soon as you read the first words of the first poem in the book you will find yourself required to think about one of the oldest and most central questions having to do with poetry: What kind of language is appropriate for the writing of poems? Ought a poem's language to be elevated, or should it be casual? Should it be intricate, or direct? Should it to at least some degree play with standard syntax and grammar, or should it be written according to accepted conventions? Here's how *Inventorys* begins:

CANTING;   MARGIN;   GINGHAM;

QUADRUPED;   FUTURE HEIRLOOM;

TRELLIS;   GLASS DECANTER

If you're anything like me, you read those words and feel both excited and worried: Excited because the poet has obviously put real thought into their language, and worried because the stakes seem immediately higher than they might seem were the language of the poem more conventional. Has the poet created difficulties with their language they will not be able to overcome?

Well, no, they haven't. Creely meets the challenge of those first lines again and again in *Inventorys*. More than that, they discover and implement, as the book unfolds, a voice that is both intellectually challenging and emotionally engaging, and again give the lie to that immortal, mistaken notion that the head and heart can't work simultaneously—and even together!—fully and successfully. *Inventorys* rewards thinking and re-thinking, reading and re-reading, as all poetry must if it is to meet that ineffable hunger for poetry all readers of poems know, which cannot finally be sated, though it can be pleased. *Inventorys* pleases that hunger.
—citation of Shane McCrae, judge of the 2022 Omnidawn Open Poetry Contest and author of *Pulling the Chariot of the Sun*

INVENTORYS

© Copyright Sam Creely, 2025. All rights reserved.

Cover design by Jeff Pethybridge
Cover typeface: Charter

Interior design by Sophia Carr and Laura Joakimson
Interior typeface: Charter and Garamond Premiere Pro

Library of Congress Cataloging-in-Publication Data

Names: Creely, Sam, 1989- author.
Title: Inventorys / Sam Creely.
Description: Oakland, California : Omnidawn Publishing, 2025.
| Summary: "In this work of hybrid historiography, Sam Creely
modulates the English sentence to map the ways anglophone imperial
self-fashioning moves in and out of social coherence, investigating
how syntactic requirements reflect colonial history and how the rules
of language structure thought. Through scenes including intimate
encounters with dye, fabric, and garments, Creely reveals the sexual and
racial grammars of empire. Inventorys takes as its point of departure the
voyage, shipwreck, and eventual excavation of the Spanish trade vessel El
Nuevo Constante. Animated by the image of sixty thousand pounds of
dye bleeding into the Gulf of Mexico, this six-part poetic documentation
follows the wreckage of the Constante linguistically, moving among early
modern lexicography, and ultimately toward enmeshed histories of catalog,
fabrication, and revision"-- Provided by publisher.

Identifiers: LCCN 2024013047 | ISBN 9781632431639 (trade paperback
Subjects: LCGFT: Poetry.
Classification: LCC PS3553.A855 O45 2024 | DDC 811/.54--dc23/
eng/20240325
LC record available at https://lccn.loc.gov/2024013047

Published by Omnidawn Publishing, Oakland, California
www.omnidawn.com
10 9 8 7 6 5 4 3 2 1
ISBN: 978-1-63243-163-9

INVENTORYS

Sam Creely

Omnidawn Publishing
Oakland, California
2025

For Jean-Thomas.

And for Rosebud.

Inventorys

CANTING;   MARGIN;   GINGHAM;

QUADRUPED;   FUTURE HEIRLOOM;

TRELLIS;   GLASS DECANTER

An item may be a collection welling from philology's

false lash, if only to the historian, or their little doweled

rocking chair on the ocean floor hoping to find a way

forward into forgetting reduce, reduce, reduce

CANTING

A thin synthetic reservoir of the had. See two figures

in crinoline advancing from animism carrying slanted

parasols. Felt surface of colloquy, teflon, polymer,

paste, put your hush finger over my mouth and tell me

time past is the only thing endless

MARGIN

It's an argument—summer thunderstorm trees

crossing lawns in a fury as if to show how nominalism

stirs from accumulation its gains and yearnings. Show me

gentleness as a tall uninvisible being, breathing out

and in yolk, powder, wax, interleaf

GINGHAM

Tablecloth, apron, button-down (not suitable, why

wear a tablecloth), or sundress (somehow suitable,

why not wear a tablecloth). Loss is a fulfillment

of privacy, narratives ordered in a long line

artifacts brick, semaphore tower, fiberglass

QUADRUPED

I like zinnias.

No not zinnias.

I like

I guess zinnias.

Mordant, horsehair, independence, adjective

FUTURE HEIRLOOM

Paly go r sk ite. Matchwoodde flinders all ok

seachops ok faint ingrauing. Even if we agree accident

makes ghosts of somatic logic or I suppose oops

here they come now hematite, masonite, instant

replay

TRELLIS

Wreck, or suggestions of wreck. Here were the notices

"Rotary grant," "In hanced," "Appeared in water stain."

In the kindred, the elision. In ephemera, the wish to be

kept. Divide water from water as if exposure did not

require intervention

GLASS DECANTER

In a particular way

      has moved me to   Because of

I can't.

     My

Fabrication fading to amber resin feather in glyph,

petal, petal, whisper:

                    whalebone bodice, go back

for your body

Excursion

not evil or pain here, it is blank here, for reasons
Walt Whitman

    Many sins are committed here and it is all
    because of cochineal
    Tlaxcalan town council

       A Rush of
       Cochineal
       Emily Dickinson

T he cochineal is waxy. A red tropical beetle whose Spanish name is at once *fine grain* and *money*, they are tiny insects who feed on the florid cactus berries of the Opuntia; they are gluttonous. Red travels through their small bodies in quantities nearly half their own weight, becoming a glucose acid that can be harvested as a colorant. If seen at a distance, a cactus with trace stripes of cochineal seems to be wounded and bleeding.

In sixteenth- and seventeenth-century Mexico, dried cochineal was the second most valued export after silver. By 1553, local officials in Oaxaca had declared the insect a source of social unrest, filing complaints that residents had stopped producing enough staple crops, leaving agrarian fields fallow. Spain's monopoly on colonial trade routes had been secure since the establishment of the Casa de

Contratación in 1503, along with a ban ordered on the export of live insects. Many merchants tried to lift this prohibition or circumvent it by smuggling live cochineal on cactus paddles disguised as light blocks of dried copal resin.

One attempt may have been made late in 1766 aboard the Spanish frigate El Nuevo Constante, part of an annual fleet that traversed the Atlantic between Veracruz and the port of Cádiz. Less than a week into its return voyage from Mexico, El Nuevo Constante ran into a hurricane and sank, plunging over a thousand lengths of dyewood and greater quantities of indigo, cochineal, and annatto into the Gulf of Mexico. The ship's manifest reads as a threnody for its most potent form of currency.

Between constant new and new constant, how do we read the stowaway prophecy carried in the ship's endemic name? The eighteenth-century rescue of the Nuevo Constante's crew took two months and six different ships. Another fleet of small vessels, descending on the site two hundred and thirteen years later, salvaged a number of plain leather sacks remarkably intact, though empty—stained with red.

Listen history's rhythm: wreck and recovery. I prepare the Constante's voyage and late twentieth-century excavation as a forecast unsettling the early modern fantasy of the universal. Invention gathers in lapses. Recall sixty thousand pounds of color swirling the depths of a gulf.

Rush of

Incursion

I tried to lift *A* threnody with gathers of light. ordered on the Gulf of a rescue where fallow form took *reasons* over the hurricane and became florid and Many. stowaway history is plain. Seen If *all* Listen.

at The seems trace *blank* into thousand thousand Another

Captain have leaves of copal

have carpets Urcullu to lull

sackcloth caucus or oakum hogan

Potlatch forage for

becomes a gettynge

Fledch mainmast against dawn

pawse pitch in fastening

Lost convoy near Balize

cinta rift wrapt en c he eh

vassal rosin chizzel

Domingo Umarán Mast

Marinar sayt buckle

    waiste him

    in promt

    he buckle

Wrest send

paragrafs of Rosebud

slow en let crowch a tothe by

near ah well sturdy puling

what spilt of its depthe

Virago sleeve in indiffrent condition

scraped lettinge long harmscye

long Cooper & Calker & Carpentar

not that harm, right harm

table lain napkins & etc articulations such as

our coppers our cashews our hammocks our capes

        Baptista Second pilot knew he

        could be the moon when askd

        how have you slept

        sound opened

        his trade language mouth

        to speak achieued only grease

        & two goatskins

Lost imprecise reproductions

won thresh vanish mackinaw

First own then own own

Vacant Boatswain

Classical rational harrow

Lacuna become wheat

from creel en throstle frame

    fathom in half retrospect

    carryed by sounds

Olympic principles

fabric & fiteing strides

 Holly at this season?

early Movement for duel

go massiue   usual other

Vague session spinning in ethic next ethic

Historic incentive

win win win

Invisible vestibule

　　rush mayde of　ox　air

lace Chaplain felt

focused forgetting

obtaned to a poynt

plainer than a sol

poring down in

logograph &

stammring:

23,750 coins mint silver

2,600 coins mint gold

10,627 lbs cochineal powdered & wild

2,896 lbs indigo

220,000 vanillas

2,439 lbs cacao soconusco

220 lbs   from caracas

60,492 lbs jalap

5,440 lbs annatto

192 lbs balsam

50 lbs powder of oaxaca

6,709 lbs sabadilla

1,032 dyewoods

125 lbs resin

2,375 tanned hides

759 knives

2 boxes chocolate

1 chest medicines

Herd a sliver of the ship's hull

Herd twice of a gloamynge

Herd three slots in bilge widing

Herd red mists risen from rockpor

Herd a golem washt upon shore hands

      bounde & bracing

Herd owre own menne caryed thunders

      & lyghtenynges about hem

Herd the choke of a barrier

Herd the waiste of a bathing sailor

Herd the sulk of a notion

Distant historic fantasy

(found under

   Rush of

distinguished by silver

thred in his slevage)

Distant historic fantasy

(everybody wore baleen)

September 4

Hurry the Clerk! they say they

    we sayl past Can-Pech

    A motione my hushe—

inspect nonattendance or

leger of the anywon else

Unseeing lesse favered or chose than

vivid realme of the noummenal

wring as it is in it self now

soothing its heave

    the task is

inventory

September 5

yd owt on that dec in bac,

al her al heir—ys for godsake

from the port but the wynd

seethinge staid three days

n pelt int hushe

               A motione my silents

not absents

strictest sistem a logicke of trading

September 7

Cochineal cradel me

or wache out your life

that theese may take

& shiver just to know it

Another
Room :

Low Hammering

Sounds
In Coppers

    Erroneous
    cordon

    Vertical
    still

    It is not
    into

    that breath
    goes

    eyes
    pushed away

    Maybe not
    pushed

so much
as held

Nymphaea
above water

while beating
careful

physiognomies
float on

Pendulant

1

He was crooked on the bed—his face squished into the flimsy pillow and his neck in a painful way. He leveled himself, but the book fell.

Mercifully centered to a disc on the ceiling, the hanging lamp swayed lightly, waffled in his room, and the boat careened now around this wave, now that. The boat leveled itself, but the hanging lamp

2

He was crooked on the bed—face squished into the pillow and his neck in a painful way. He corrected himself, but the book fell.

The hanging lamp was centered to a disc on the ceiling, and it swayed lightly, waffled in the room, and the boat careening now around this wave, now that. The boat corrected itself, but the lamp remained crooked. It frightened him. Restless, his focus was unable

3

The lamp was centered on the ceiling and it swayed lightly,

the boat careening now around this wave, now that. The boat
corrected itself, but the lamp, when it & it was a hanging lamp

Restless his eyes rolled about the room: the bed the bottles &

the crooked lamp the tapestry & the crooked lamp the luggage

4

    bed bottles

tapestry luggage shoes ship in a bottle — If frightened

                                                           to

    always fell

    Frightened & he began to despair: not the lamp at all! the floor, the ceiling, the walls, the furniture ~~The t~~

5

The truth of the crookedness of the lamp made obvious the falsehood of the correctness of the room. *The floor, the ceiling, the walls, he wailed, the furniture, my whole existence—all are crookedness!*

The fact that a room is not always the truth made him doubt of the truth of any room at any time, & from there onward had to discover for himself what a room was saying and whether it was crooked or correct. Sometimes he could figure out that it was not correct by watching a hanging lamp for example, or by placing a glass of water on the floor & watching the angle of the water in the glass—but how was he ever to know that it was not crooked? Perhaps crooked & correct did not matter. Still he would like to know, if only for clarity

6

The fact that a room is not always the truth made him uncertain of the truth of any room at any time, and now he must discover for himself what a room is saying and whether it is crooked or correct. It was not a phantasmagoria. Dawn pawing the hem of his skirt and

Slow Rosebud

with a Blonde push
Over your impotence
Emily Dickinson

with the final vowel dragged out and aspirated,
Eduardo Kohn

Her shoulder nestles itself, fleets

of monks inventing the tassel

not as a cumulation but as a compounding

grass where there used to be cactus

that kind of fakery

Who could I tell? Already bursting violet pink

when the pinch is as old as the borrow

So many yarn

Her shoulder nestles itself, alloy
in thin phoneme. Stockpile rinding
queer as a stereograph

Fenceline swept back in winter
What are the nine parts?

Sibilant wing oh it must be
I'm old, probably
threadbare

Yes, fluke, we cause pleasures too

O tiose how the limbs go at it
you know the sense of straining through wire
the thin scorching oh lord of the proscenium
its lip too close, so seeable

What do we learn we learn to notice
in the nape of the neck, a remnant
in the small of the back, pre-crisis

Ealdnysse,
(throe simmer of hinder)
fills a teacup with port
says take, you
take. Off we go
grandmother wherever
you are in time

O.A. Bullard portrait of the Dickinson children, 1840

The space of desire is identified by lace
Or Emily in velvet again suited to January light
less lambent Placing lace

In some sustained present, three children sit for a portrait in
Amherst eyes deep-set and focused, look-stamped

By one plate while mortared pronominal
A likeness, believe me, without

>   Emily left, cleft
>   chin and hair cropped
>   in that "free" style

Extends her left hand, flashes a pink moss rose
and its notion Her to herself in form
bold, as the Chestnut Burr—Would this do as well?

Slow Rosebud

1

Vocation in profile
a flat fold, a doubling

White plait down her back
Wet bearded rye

Texture enters perception

drifts along flagstone
in linen

2

She sits in expanding silhouette
in the bathtub washing her hair

Nopal cactus

Lucid green unblooming
(too much water)

Winnow, breathe for me

　　　　tuché　　*tathātā*

3

Windswept deciduous interval
Rosebud and southernwood

Tossing coins into the drift

Generations slacken
Language un-tariffed returning

         to language

Thrum strung some

4

From the sky there is no
trace of dimension

Example of a roll of twine

Zoom in and the dot becomes a sphere
Closer,   becomes thread
Closer,   becomes cylinder
Closer,   becomes fiber

Tiny twisting lines

This old woman bent
over in fields of annatto

5

Fabric pressed flat holds
memory of dimension

Example of pleating silk

If the bound acts as a problem of resist
If the pressure exerted by thread
If over and under exposure
tending their traces

Shadow accidents

A hyacinth grown out of her hands

6

Red enough for forgetting
we hefted forms of replica

readied our palms

       Best cactus is seen cactus

7

Red enough for forgetting

The search began with a barrier

The word for motion is delay

8

The search began with a barrier
White viscid buckram

Sharks in

Way of contour even in winter then

9

The word for motion is delay

A terry sock left in the pantry
(Rosebud below)

Scatter syntax
first ended then remembered

these spots of blood on a plotline

Jupiter

the ship began to work its way into the mud, gradually settling until the ship began to work
its way into the mud, gradually settling until   the ship began to work its way into the mud,
gradually setting until the ship

mud, gradually settling

work its way into

settling until the

work its way

gradually

the ship

work its

the mud,

settling

ship began

way into

gradually

until the

to work its

mud, gradually

ship began to work

mud, gradually settling

work its way into the mud,

ship began to work its way into the

began to work its way into the

until the ship began to

the mud, gradually

ship began to

into the mud,

settling until

began to

way into

gradually

until the

to work its

the mud,

settling

ship began

way into the

settling until the

its way into the

until the ship began to

gradually settling until the

mud, gradually settling until the ship

began to work its way into the mud, gradually settling until the ship began to work its way
into the mud, gradually settling until the ship began to work its way into the mud,
gradually settling until the ship began to work its way into the mud, gradually

The Queen

To set a Vat of twelve Barrels.

(Late first light.)
 (On a river rock holding a dagger.)

QUIET
 (Posing for Pity in broadcloth,
 whispers.)

What is wind from wind's perspective?

run your cloth...
air, and run again;

craft and plying   frock

What is its texture?

(Long light gust seeking unforming.)

(Held in melding color.)

crossstitch in
vellum arrival

Courses around it.

Yellow and Blue

BLUE gloaming tendrils of sunshade hang
downward in ports of importance now Rosebud converging
in blue even in her own marbled semidarkness even in terrycloth
there are aspects of her life some people would like to hear about ok
here is a blanket here is a cigarette honey this Beauvais tapestry hasn't
exactly gotten on with the elements ok here is the side you were never
meant to see here is America with eyes bent evolved from her standard
sixteenth century depictions no clothes battle axe astride an armadillo
now demurred covered in blue patterned azure blue to fall through

if she started with an idea of YELLOW a gentle
wringing somewhere deep in the patio furniture or a sense of
sunrise hand draped over amber one strong jaw and a heavy pattern with
recently drawn drape recently cut hair and a scent of mandarin oh she
knows very well about adding milk to citrus since that time in the blue
kitchenette knows very well who she was when she drew it less of who
she was in the moments that followed not the slightest notion where she
bought this dress or where her grandson has run off to tile beneath her
gives way to lawn where maybe her daughter maybe even the same dress
shop picnics together and there comes running right at her at her or the
fig tree in summer straw hat and sailor stripes raps his head on a branch

From Dignity

The light is distributed by thin metal Begin with a light
bent thin as the disc of a notion glides toward and
presses against the other disc of the something it
might become now one sprouting silver-
grained aberrance Arrange the discs
along one axis *taxonomy* Two or
more discs *tautology* Move the
discs together *hermeneutics*
Move the discs apart
teleology   Pull
back   the
leaves

        If she could
sit in silence, hide
here   as   in   air,
rushing,   on   on
until the first small
wist   of   a   cloud
emerged,   almost
aim,   almost
motion, on and on.
        Eventually
language   issues,
slips   into   other
language,   each
word a clear plastic
envelope, the kind
with a button that
snaps.   "There,"
she   said,   possibly
actually,   possibly
audibly,   spurring
the   bathwater   to
take   up   its   falling
away

Tend

While talking to Grandmother, tend her house.

Center the Austrian dish.

Water the ferns.

Stack the jars of turmeric in either cupboard.

Empty the yellow pitcher of rain.

Arrange camellias in a vase, rinse the vase, it would be
a good plan to have remembered that in advance.

Remove dental floss from the bed linens.

Do not touch the cobalt glasses or the jardiniere.

Do not open the blinds.

You can fetch the yellow pitcher.

More or less quiet, she says, *used to be such noise in*
the summer now there isn't, eating a carrot, making
thin bone breaking sounds with her teeth.

Consider "novels devoted to influenza."

Wax mahogany in the hall.

What gathers behind words as they move into quiet,
how heavy how creased.

Remove dental floss from the banister in the stairway.

"...poems to typhoid; odes to pneumonia; lyrics to tooth-ache."
Virginia Woolf points out that while language can express
the interior life of Hamlet's mind, Lear "has no words for
the shiver and the headache."

Polish the knob to the closet in the guest room.

Dust the casing.

Grease the hinges.

This fence in the lawn between care and not caring whose is it.

Level the door.

Behind it is a space where no one walks.

The carpet here is still blue.

Take out her robe à l'anglaise.

Ask: what about this dress invites the narrative,

"Era: Victorian."

Silk from Macau.

Acapulco annatto, granilla.

Met in Manila, through Borneo, Sumatra.

Stitching tendencies French.

Yardage Gujarati.

North American neckline.

Up with the lace.

Tighten the crinoline.

Fasten its clasps in the window at sunrise.

Walk in then back out from invention.

Stay awhile.

Acknowledgments

My deep gratitude to Shane McCrae for selecting this manuscript—
and to Rusty Morrison, Laura Joakimson, and Sophia Carr for your
collaborative ethos and steadfast support and guidance throughout
the production process. Jeffrey Pethybridge, thank you for the
beautiful cover design and for ruminating with me on styles of
legibility and illegibility.

My utmost thanks are to Douglas Kearney and Jon Wagner, who
read more drafts than I can remember, and whose various pedagogies
continue to point the way.

This book exists thanks to many acts of friendship, mentorship,
conversation, kindness, and close reading over many years. Thank
you Annie Render, Lyle Kash, Michael Davidson, Tisa Bryant,
Anthony McCann, Robin Coste Lewis, Ana Cecilia Alvarez, Rosa
Boshier González, Alyssa Manansala, Indigo Weller, Harry Dodge,
Mike Bryant, Amanda Choo Quan, Sophie Reiff, Gio Alonzi, Leann
Lo, Sara Selevitch, Vanessa Baish, Mimi Haddon, Jen Hofer, Brian
Evenson, Alecia Menzano, Sarah Naim, Cynthia Velásquez, Jess
Goldschmidt, Yuxin Zhao, Michelle McLaughlin, Dany Naierman,
Paola Escobar, Melu Waingarten, Santos Arrué, Tim Nicholas, Alexa
Best, Allison Yasukawa, Gabrielle Civil, Jules Gill-Peterson, Kate
Ladenheim, Melody Ling, Rebecca LeCroix, Shona Tritt, Rebecca
Lock, Brooke Bastie, David Cecchetto, Dan Guadagnolo, and Shama
Rangwala.

Pia Sazani, you get your own line. Thank you for the long collaboration.

Much appreciation to my colleagues and co-teachers Elizabeth Chin, Mashinka Firunts Hakopian, Rocío Carlos, Ben Hooker, and Maggie Hendrie.

To my longtime friends Arpana Arjun, Amy Jacobson, Michael Rooney, Rowan Darko, Elizabeth Nearing, Taylor Reynolds, Megan Spatz, Juliacks, and Miranda Steege, thank you.

To Rochelle and Fred Rosen, may time past be endless.

To Michael Creely, who taught me form.

To Amy Rosen, by whom I know literature.

Finally, I thank Jean-Thomas Tremblay, my partner, my favorite writer and character. For your intellect and constant love, and for convincing me to publish before ninety. If I make it that long, may it be with you.

Sam Creely is an Assistant Professor at ArtCenter College of Design. With Pia Sazani, they are a founding editor of DanceNotes Chaplet Series and co-author of *Throat Draw Come Out With It* (2023). *Inventorys* is their debut poetry collection.

Inventorys

by Sam Creely

Cover design by Jeff Pethybridge
Cover typeface: Charter
Interior design by Sophia Carr and Laura Joakimson
Interior typeface: Charter and Garamond Premier Pro

Printed in the United States by Books International,
Dulles, Virginia on Acid Free Archival Quality Recycled Paper
Publication of this book was made possible in part by gifts from
Katherine & John Gravendyk in honor of Hillary Gravendyk,
Francesca Bell, Mary Mackey, and The New Place Fund

Omnidawn Publishing Oakland, California
Staff and Volunteers, Spring 2025
Rusty Morrison & Laura Joakimson, co-publishers
Rob Hendricks, poetry & fiction editor,
& post-pub marketing
Jeffrey Kingman, copy editor
Sharon Zetter, poetry editor & book designer
Anthony Cody, poetry editor
Liza Flum, poetry editor
Rayna Carey, poetry editor
Sophia Carr, production editor
Elizabeth Aeschliman, fiction & poetry editor
Jennifer Metsker, marketing assistant
Avantika Chitturi, marketing assistant
Angela Liu, marketing assistant